Getting Your Second Wind: Living a Smoke-Free Life

A Kid's Guide to Saying No to Smoking

By
Teresea A. Mathis, Ed.S., LMSW
Counselor
Columbia, SC

Susan J. Smith-Rex, Ed.D.
Professor of Special Education
Richard W. Riley College of Education
Winthrop University
Rock Hill, SC

Sara C. Castillo, Ph.D.
Child Clinical Psychologist
Catawba Family Center
Rock Hill, SC

Illustrations coordinated by Ruthann Maunéy
Front Cover drawing by Justin Rivenbark

Production editor—

Don L. Sorenson, Ph.D.

Graphic Design—

Earl Sorenson

Illustrators—

Students at Northwestern High School in Rock Hill, South Carolina

Jennifer Anthony	Joe Blanton	Jamie Busby
Kristie Demarest	Archie Fallon	Chris Gervais
Angela Jordan	Jenny Kilbourne	Rachel Lee
Robbie Leslie	Jacob McCann	Shea Payne
Justin Rivenbark	Kyle Saverance	Nikki Scoggins
Amy Starnes	Danielle Sweetapple	John Thomas
Kristin Timmerman	Catlin Werrell	

Teresea Mathis, Ed.S, LMSW; Susan Smith-Rex, Ed.D.; and Sara Castillo, Ph.D.

Table of Contents

Note to Parents and Health Professionals:

This book is intended to aid children to say "No" to smoking. It was carefully written to be user friendly for children. We trust the vocabulary, illustrations, and limited number of words on each page will make this book inviting and helpful to children in their understanding of making good choices.

The second part of this book focuses on practical ideas children can use to better cope with the temptation to smoke. The student selects areas of concern and completes the activities which will help the child explore what needs to be done to best cope.

Suggestions to parents, administrators, teachers, and counselors are provided in part three. While the book can be used independently by upper elementary and middle school students, we highly recommend parents, teachers, counselors, and mental health professionals read and discuss this book with children. In this way, suggestions are fully discussed and the children are encouraged to follow through with the coping strategies provided.

Best wishes as you put this book to good use!

Teresea A. Mathis, Ed.S., LMSW

Susan J. Smith-Rex, Ed.D.

Sara C. Castillo, Ph.D.

Part I

Helping Children Live a Smoke-Free Life

Shea Payne

Most children, when they are in elementary school, have a strong dislike of cigarette smoking. Kids do not like it when their parents smoke and they make sure their parents know how they feel.

Danielle Sweetapple

Kids usually do not like the smell of smoke. It makes their house and clothes smell bad; it causes the smoker to have bad breath, yellow teeth, wrinkles, thick and brittle nails; and it can make breathing uncomfortable.

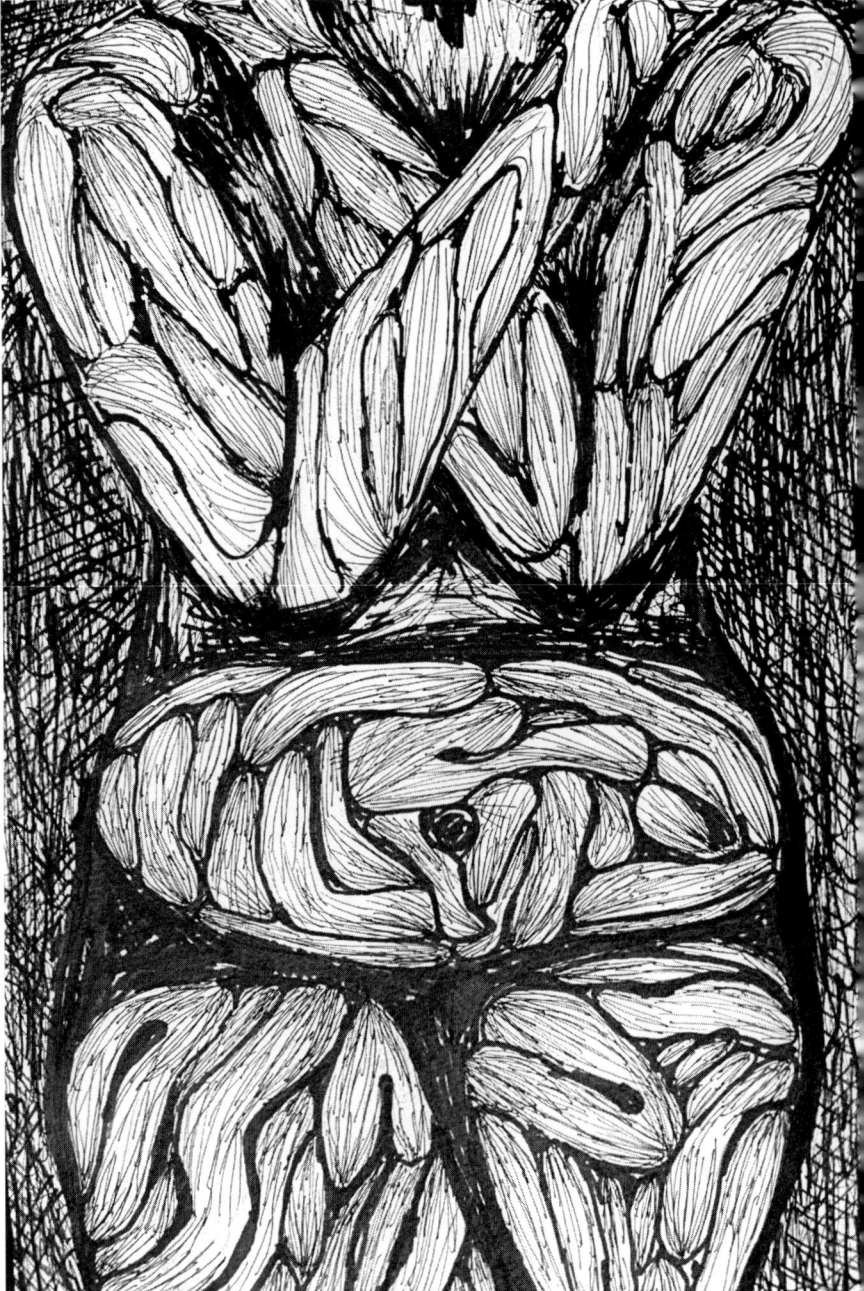

Catlin Werrell

Kids learn in their health classes facts about smoking that further strengthens their hope that the people they care about will quit smoking. Some of these facts are:

- *Cigarette smoke contains 4000 chemical compounds (43 are carcinogens and over 200 are known poisons).*

- *Smoking has been linked to 11 separate types of cancer.*

- *One person dies of tobacco-induced disease every 13 seconds.*

- *Smoking makes it harder to fight colds, coughs, and headaches.*

- *Asthma is the most common chronic illness in children and it is worse when a child is in a smoke-filled room.*

Jacob McCann

*Believing at an early age the negative health risks of smoking, why is it that some kids cannot fight off the **urge** to experiment with smoking? We must help kids to recognize the reasons why they may be tempted to smoke, as well as the many reasons why they should resist this temptation.*

Kristin Timmerman

Many factors contribute to why young people choose to smoke:
- *The addictive quality of nicotine.*
- *The role of advertising.*
- *The influence of friends and family.*
- *The need to experiment.*
- *The search for a self-image.*

Shea Payne

The nicotine in cigarettes is as addictive and as potentially dangerous as heroin. One out of every five deaths in the United States is linked to nicotine addiction. Why would anyone consider taking a chance at becoming an addict?

Joe Blanton

It can take as few as fifteen cigarettes to become addicted to nicotine.

- *Physical addictions can happen in just one week.*
- *Emotional addictions can be as strong as chemical addictions (holding the cigarette, hanging with the crowd, believing one looks older, feeling "flirty").*

Teresea Mathis, Ed.S, LMSW; Susan Smith-Rex, Ed.D.; and Sara Castillo, Ph.D.

Kyle Saverance

Tobacco is often called the "gateway drug." This is because it often leads to other addictive behaviors.

- *Teens who smoke are three times more likely than nonsmokers to use alcohol.*

- *Teens who smoke are eight times more likely to use marijuana.*

- *Teens who smoke are three times more likely to see a doctor for an emotional complaint.*

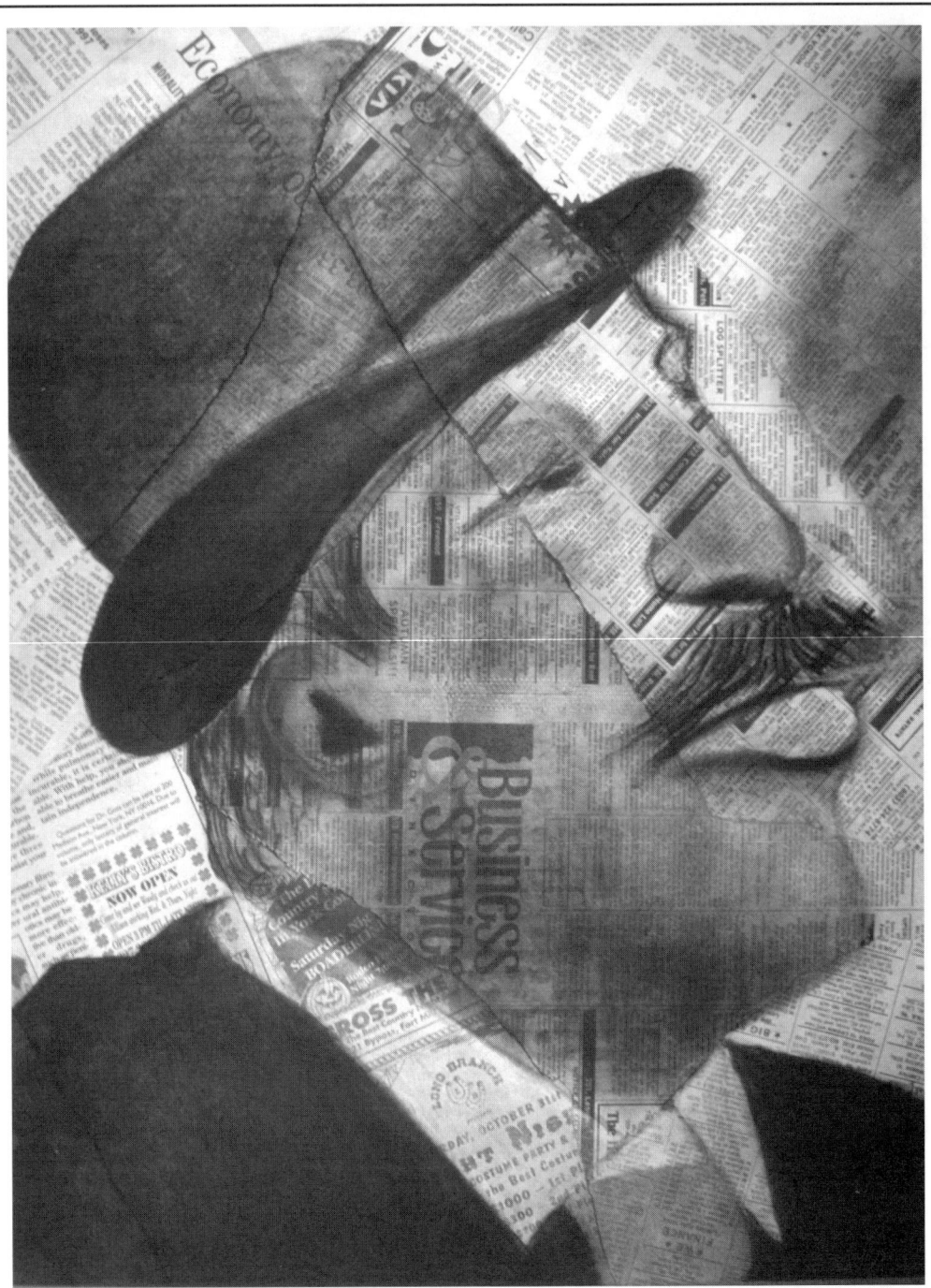

Jennifer Anthony

When your grandparents were teenagers and young adults, there was little evidence that smoking caused life-threatening diseases. In 1946 was the first mention that smoking might be related to cancer.

Teresea Mathis, Ed.S, LMSW; Susan Smith-Rex, Ed.D.; and Sara Castillo, Ph.D.

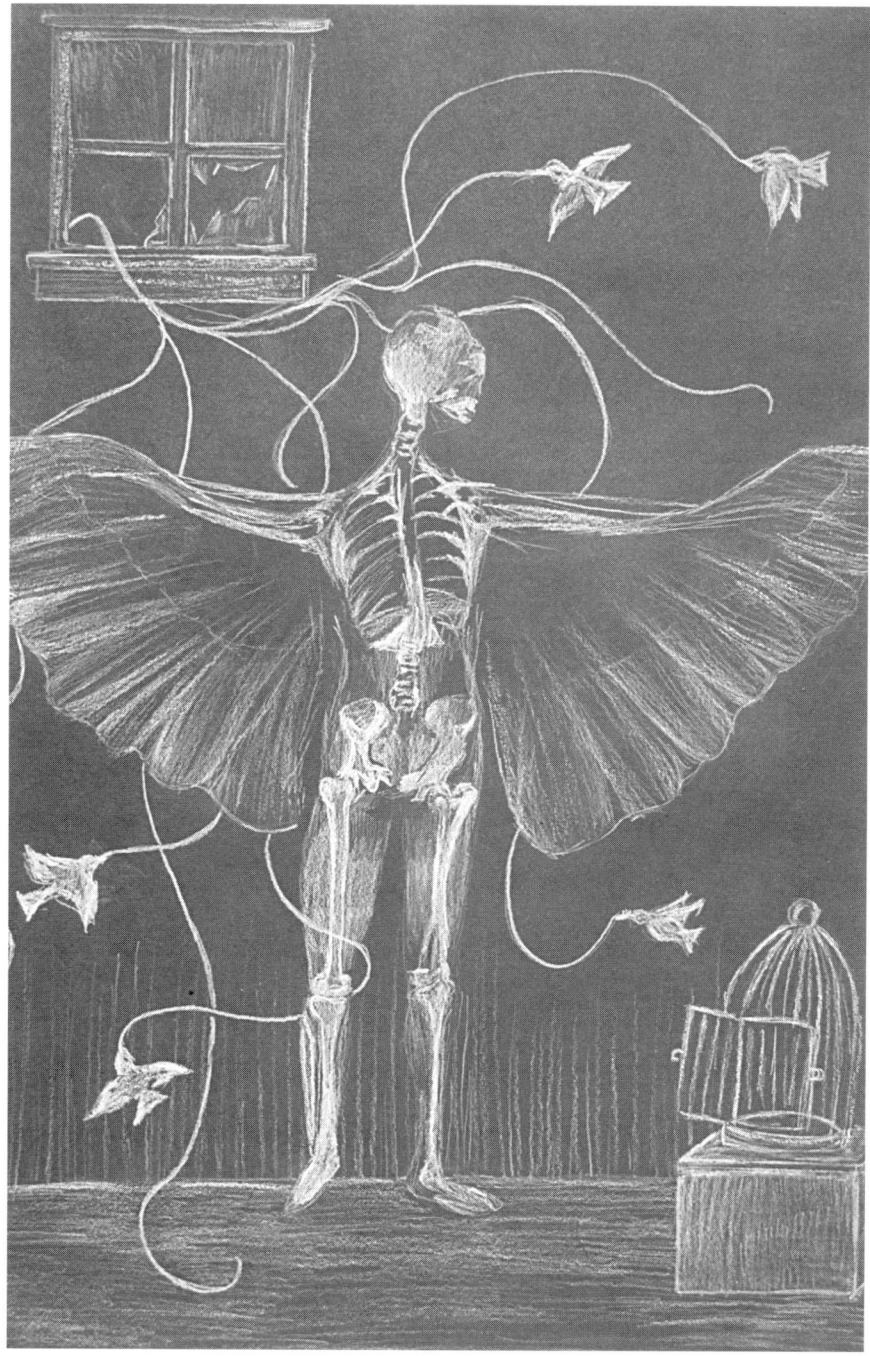

Catlin Werrell

Unfortunately, young folks have watched their elderly loved ones die early from health complications such as:

- *Cancer*
- *Heart disease*
- *Emphysema*
- *Chronic bronchitis*
- *Ulcers*

Archie Fallon

Because cigarette smoking is so addictive, it is important to not experiment with this habit. Even though people think they can quit the habit whenever they decide the urge is over, it isn't that easy. Children go through withdrawal symptoms that make "kicking the habit" very hard to do. Of the daily smokers who think that they will not smoke in five years, nearly seventy-five percent are still smoking five years later.

Chris Gervais

It is illegal for anyone under 18 years old to purchase tobacco, and yet, in the past, the tobacco industry hoped teenagers would find smoking attractive and eventually make it a lifetime habit. Animals, cartoons, and gimmicks were often used in advertisements to attract teenagers in order to replace the 3,000 smokers who die or quit each day.

Jenny Kilbourne

Here are some common advertisement strategies used by the tobacco industry.

- *A famous person is shown smoking.*
- *A good looking person is shown smoking.*
- *Parties and adventure are associated with smoking.*
- *Advertisements suggest smoking will make you thin, independent, and successful.*
- *Most ads show young people having fun.*

Kristie Demarest

Television and movies can sometimes glamorize smoking to young folks. It may appear that smoking makes you look "cool," important, or powerful. In the past tobacco companies were spending thirteen million dollars a day on advertising to make sure people connected smoking with being beautiful, confident, thin, and attractive.

Joe Blanton

*Consider these statistics before you choose to even **try** smoking:*

- *More than half of all smokers begin smoking before the age of fourteen.*

- *The younger people start smoking cigarettes, the more likely they are to become strongly addicted to nicotine.*

- *Virtually everyone who smokes starts while in high school.*

- *Eighty percent of smokers become addicted before they turn eighteen.*

- *Of the 3000 kids that begin smoking every day, statistics indicate that 750 will die due to smoking-related illnesses.*

Kristie Demarest

Everyday 3000 more teens pick up the habit of smoking. Smoking-related illnesses kill more Americans each year than heroin, cocaine, alcohol, AIDS, fires, homicides, suicides, and traffic accidents combined!

*About one third of our high school teenagers in the United States smoke cigarettes and yet seven out of every ten teens who become addicted to smoking will tell you that they **really** regret ever starting this habit.*

Read the following eight testimonials:

Testimonials

Zack is 15 years old

My grandfather had a heart attack and now he has cancer. Don't try smoking! Stay away from people who are going to ask you to do things you're not supposed to do.

Blake is 15 years old

I hate smoking. I saw what it did to my dad's side of the family. They spend all of their money on cigarettes and alcohol. It lowers your standards.

Chris is 15 years old

Nobody has control over anyone else. I did it because I was curious. You can't know what to expect. If you start smoking, you will regret it.

Caleb is 16 years old

Curiosity is probably the only reason you would start smoking, but that's not good enough.

English is 16 years old

I can't do sports. I get tired so easily. You go through a stage when you want to try everything. Don't try smoking! I thought I could quit if I wanted to, but I can't.

Judy is 15 years old

I started smoking to be defiant to my parents. I didn't hurt them; I hurt myself. Kids need to know more about the habit before a decision is made. The government should keep raising the price of cigarettes and the cops should arrest store employees who sell them to minors.

Drew is 15 years old

Once you start it is really hard to stop. You're always hiding. It screws up your life.

Craigen is 14 years old

There is no point to smoking. It affects your health and makes problems worse. It affects your attitude and family life.

Archie Fallon

Research tells us that a young smoker who becomes an addicted smoker and smokes two packs of cigarettes a day has a life expectancy which is eight years shorter than a nonsmoker.

Angela Jordan

*It is hard to be **truly** concerned about those eight extra years when you're a teenager, but try asking elderly relatives whom you love if they would like to have eight extra years added to their lives and see what they say.*

Teresea Mathis, Ed.S, LMSW; Susan Smith-Rex, Ed.D.; and Sara Castillo, Ph.D.

John Thomas

What are some of the reasons why adults say they smoke? Here are some of the most common excuses:

- *I have family members who smoke.*

- *It relaxes me.*

- *I smoke to control my weight.*

- *I smoke to be more sociable.*

- *I smoke when I am bored.*

- *I feel so addicted that I can't stop the powerful urge.*

Nikki Scoggins

What are some of the reasons why young teenagers start smoking?
- *I want to look older.*
- *I want to lose weight.*
- *I think it looks "cool."*
- *I smoke because I am bored or lonely.*
- *I want to "fit in" with other kids.*
- *I want to rebel against my parents, school, or society.*
- *I want to relieve anger or stress.*

Smart students don't throw their money away on a dirty, destructive habit like smoking. Let's do some math!

If a pack of cigarettes costs $3.00 and you smoke a pack a day, how much will you need to support your habit every week?

$3.00 x 7 days = _____

How much money would you waste in a year?

_____ x 52 weeks = _____

Let's do some comparison shopping! If you saved the money you would have spent on cigarettes, you would have over $1,000.00 per year to invest in something meaningful.

Spend $1,000.00 in other ways:

How many CDs could you buy? _____

How many pairs of shoes could you buy? _____

How many movies could you see? _____

Amy Starnes

Kristin Timmerman

Research tells us that a teenager's body reacts to smoking in some negative ways.

- *The heart rates of young smokers are two to three beats per minute faster than nonsmokers.*

- *Students show a reduction in memory skills.*

- *Students are more likely to suffer from depression and have some emotional problems.*

- *Students have more headaches, colds, coughs, and flu.*

- *Students tend to have lower grades and get into more trouble at school.*

- *It takes as few as fifteen cigarettes to become addicted to nicotine. Physical addiction can happen in just one week.*

> **Warning:** *Cigarettes are not problem solvers. Your problems will still be there whether you smoke or not. You are the only one who can tackle the problems.*

Although smoking even one cigarette causes a lot of damage, the effects can be countered if the person **chooses** *to quit smoking.*

- *One year after quitting smoking, the excess risk of heart disease is cut in half.*
- *After fifteen years of a smoke-free life, the risk is similar to a person who never smoked.*

Robbie Leslie

*Smoking is a stimulant, **but** it lasts for a very short time. Cigarettes will **not** give you a long relaxing feeling. If you want to ease tension and feel more relaxed, get some exercise. Here are some of the benefits of exercise:*

- *Gives you more energy.*
- *Helps in coping with stress.*
- *Improves your self-image.*
- *Helps prevent depression.*
- *Helps you to relax.*
- *Improves your ability to fall asleep quickly and sleep well.*
- *Gives you an easy way to meet new friends.*
- *Increases muscle strength.*
- *Helps your heart and lungs work more efficiently.*

Angela Jordan

Listed below are good aerobic activities:

- *Dancing*
- *Bicycling*
- *Hiking*
- *Jogging*
- *Jumping rope*
- *Swimming*
- *Walking briskly*
- *Basketball*
- *Calisthenics*
- *Racquetball*
- *Tennis*
- *Soccer*
- *Volleyball*
- *Stair-climbing*

Rachel Lee

Don't forget about second hand smoke. If you aren't convinced to not smoke for your own health, consider doing it for someone else. Second hand smoke kills about three thousand nonsmokers each year due to lung cancer.

Kyle Saverance

Smoking is the single most preventable cause of death in our society, and yet cigarettes are the only legal product in America that, when used as intended, can cause death. Twenty-three percent of all Americans surveyed said they were in favor of outlawing cigarettes.

Teresea Mathis, Ed.S, LMSW; Susan Smith-Rex, Ed.D.; and Sara Castillo, Ph.D.

Chris Gervais

There are few teenagers who are ready to hear that their life is about to end. However, if you are going to risk your life for that cigarette, be prepared to eventually have that cigarette take your health, and maybe even your life. Instead of making a choice to smoke, make a choice to lead a smoke-free life. The following sections will help you make positive choices and learn coping skills to help you stay in control of your life.

DECISIONS

Individuality

Belonging

Persuasion

Control

GOALS

Choices

Part II

Practical Ideas to Help Say No to Smoking

Terms

Addict	A person who becomes addicted to a drug.
Addiction	When a person depends upon a drug to deal with life.
Advertising	When a company calls attention to something they wish to sell.
Aerobic activities	An exercise regimen designed to strengthen the cardiovascular system.
Anxiety	A feeling of fearful uneasiness or worry about what may happen.
Carcinogen	A term meaning "cancer-causing substances."
Chemical dependency	A strong need to use a drug, such as nicotine, to feel better about yourself or to escape from problems.
Chronic	A condition that develops slowly and results in long-lasting symptoms.
Coping skills	Positive ways to act so you can feel good about yourself and begin solving your problems.
Depression	The emotion of feeling sad, blue, and unhappy.
Nicotine	A poisonous substance found in tobacco.
Poor self-esteem	When a person feels of little or no worth.
Self-image	How a person sees or feels about himself or herself.
Smokeless tobacco	Chewing and dipping tobacco.
Stimulant	A chemical that temporarily excites bodily functions.
Strategy	A careful plan for achieving a goal.
Support system	Community helpers and family you know you can turn to for help.
Tobacco	A broad-leaved herb prepared for smoking or chewing.
Withdrawal symptoms	Signs of discomfort that tell you the body is recovering from a drug.

Learning the Facts About Smoking

1. The first mention that smoking might be related to cancer came in 1946.

2. Cigarette smoke contains over 4,000 known poisons.

3. Nicotine is a stimulant. It raises your heart rate, blood pressure, and adrenaline level, but for only a short time. One out of every five deaths in the U.S. is linked to nicotine addiction.

4. The resting heart rates of young adult smokers are two to three beats per minute faster than those of nonsmokers.

5. High school seniors who are regular smokers and begin smoking by grade nine are three times more likely to see a doctor for an emotional or psychological complaint.

6. Students who smoke show a significant reduction in retention and short-term memory than nonsmokers.

7. Thirty-six percent of high school teens in the U.S. smoke cigarettes.

8. Seven out of ten teens who become addicted to smoking say they regret ever starting.

9. Every day 3,000 more teens pick up the habit of smoking. (One thousand of each 3,000 will eventually die from a smoking related illness.)

10. According to the Center for Disease Control, 40% of white, 33% of Hispanic, and 12% of African-American female teenagers smoke, often to control their weight.

11. One person dies of tobacco-induced disease every thirteen seconds.

12. A 25-year-old smoker who smokes two packs a day has a life expectancy 8.3 years shorter than a nonsmoker.

13. Twenty-three percent of Americans are in favor of outlawing cigarettes.

Techniques of Persuasion

When reading magazines or watching TV, you have probably seen many advertisements, movies, or TV shows that are using techniques to persuade people to use and/or buy a certain product.

Here are some of the techniques used to make people think smoking is "cool" or "sexy."

1. The Bandwagon—Tries to persuade people that a large number of people smoke.

2. The Testimonial—Tries to use a famous person to persuade people by talking about smoking.

3. The Transfer—Shows a famous person smoking.

4. Emotional Appeal—Uses particular words to encourage people to have strong feelings for or against something.

5. Repetition—Repeats words over and over so people will remember them.

6. Appeal to Romance or Fantasy—A good-looking, sociable, well-dressed person using a certain product.

7. Humor—Uses something funny to promote smoking.

8. Concern for the Good of the Public—Ads which claim concern about social problems.

As you have seen above, persuasion can be negative and get you to make wrong choices.

However, there are positive persuasion techniques that are used by people who care about you and want you to do the right thing.

Parents, teachers, and good friends use persuasion to help you make good choices.

On the following pages are exercises which can help you to make good choices, feel confident about yourself, and monitor your progress.

Teresea Mathis, Ed.S, LMSW; Susan Smith-Rex, Ed.D.; and Sara Castillo, Ph.D.

Decisions – Decisions

You make decisions *everyday*. Some are easy and simple. Some are difficult. Think about the decisions you make. What or who plays a part in your decisions?

- What I have for breakfast.
- What I wear to school.
- Whether or not I do my homework.
- Who I sit with at lunch.
- Who I am with during my free time.
- What I watch on TV.
- What movies I see.
- If I do my chores.

Add other decisions here: _____

_____

Think about this. Do any of the following people influence your decisions?

- Mother
- Father
- Teacher
- Friends

If so, how and why? _____

_____

With decisions come consequences. What are the consequences?

Example:

If I do my homework:

- I will understand the material/information.
- I will make better grades.
- I will have an easier time passing tests.
- My parents will be happy and I will be able to do more things at home.

If I do *not* do my homework:

- My grades will start to fall.
- My parents will get angry and put me on restriction.

Add other reasons here:

- _____

- _____

You are in Control

You make the choice and therefore you are responsible for the outcome.

It is important to remember that you can make better choices by considering the consequences before making your decision.

Chris Gervais

This is your personal remote control.

Changer	Remember you can change your mind if you know something doesn't seem right.
Pause	Stop and think before you decide.
Menu	Evaluate all options before making your choice.
Fast Forward	In your mind, fast forward to what the consequences of your decision might be.
Rewind	Play back in your mind some decisions that didn't work out as a reminder not to make the same mistake.
Slow Motion	Remember it's okay to take your time in making important decisions.
Power	If it would not be a good decision, ***zap it!***
Play	Enjoy the benefits of your good decision.

The Good, The Bad—Your Choice

Consider decisions you have made in the past and the reasons why they were either good or bad (positive or negative).

Take a sheet of paper and divide it into two columns. Label one "Good Decisions" and the other "Bad Decisions."

Think about what causes some decisions to be good ones with positive consequences and other decisions to be bad ones with negative consequences. It is the outcome of a decision that makes it good or bad.

Think about a train moving down a track. It starts down one track, but down the way the track splits and you must decide to go one way or the other.

If you stay on one track, the train will travel past a beautiful mountain view; the other track leads into a dark tunnel and you don't know what is on the other side. It is up to you to decide which track to take. Remember, sometimes it helps to know what is at the end of the track in order to make your best decision.

Think about how you make a decision.

1. What is the decision?
2. What are your choices?
3. What are the consequences?
4. What is best for you?

Chris Gervais

How to Make the Right Decisions

1. Establish your goals. (What are your priorities? Think about your three top goals.)

2. List your choices and evaluate them. (Brainstorm every alternative you can think of and take into account personal considerations.)

3. Consider the risks and trade-offs. (Are other people a part of your decision? Can you talk to them about it? Do you really want to do it? Are you sure your decision will not hurt anyone? Is there a need to compromise in exchange for something more valuable?)

4. Evaluate your decision.

Goal → Choice → Reason → Evaluate

Goal: Resisting peer pressure to smoke.

Choice: To say no and walk away. (See page 46)

Reason: I care about my health.

Evaluate: It makes me feel good about myself, and I know good friends care about me and my health.

Goal: _____

Choice: _____

Reason: _____

Evaluate: _____

_____

Teresea Mathis, Ed.S, LMSW; Susan Smith-Rex, Ed.D.; and Sara Castillo, Ph.D.

You Are What You Think

You have heard the saying, "You are what you eat." Well, you could also say "You are what you think." Let's do a couple of exercises to help you see how this works.

This would be an example of negative thinking.

> Let's say you are getting ready for a spelling test. As you practice the words, you only focus on the ones that you get wrong. You can end up feeling like you are never going to learn the words and maybe that you are just plain stupid.

This would be an example of positive thinking.

> As you practice the words, you focus on the ones you get right and you begin making a list of the ones you have learned. With each one you learn, you add it to the list. You begin to get a feeling of accomplishment and feel you are smart.

Having a positive outlook on life can help you be optimistic and feel good about the future.

In addition to saying, "You are what you think," we could add, "You are what you do." Let's do some more exercises to see how this works.

This would be an example of negative behavior.

> You hang around with friends who smoke and use bad language. After a while you begin behaving in the same way. You think it is okay to smoke and use bad language because, after all, your friends do it too.

This would be an example of positive behavior.

> You hang around with friends who are "cool" in other ways. They respect their peers and adults. They feel making good grades are important. They enjoy having fun by going to the movies, going to eat at their favorite hangout, and spending the night at each other's homes.

Spending time in positive relationships with your friends really does lead to you having a positive outlook on life. See if you can think of other things that you think or do that impact how you live.

Examples of my own positive thinking:

_____

_____

_____

_____

_____

_____

Examples of my own positive behaviors:

_____

_____

_____

_____

_____

_____

What you think and what you do can greatly impact how you feel. The last few exercises you have done are good examples of this. Thinking positively about yourself and doing the right thing will make you feel good about yourself. Take some time to list how the positive behaviors and positive thinking you listed on the previous page made you feel.

Thinking positively makes me feel:

_____

_____

_____

_____

_____

My positive behavior makes me feel:

_____

_____

_____

_____

_____

Ways to Say No

Resisting peer pressure can be really hard. Pick five of these statements and practice saying them assertively!

- No.

- No thanks.

- My parents would put me on restriction for life.

- I don't need it.

- I don't need it to have fun.

- I'm not into body pollution.

- I get grounded if I look sideways at my kid brother. I'd hate to think what would happen if my mom caught me smoking.

- No thanks. I'm already in enough trouble with my parents.

- I'm into healthy!

- Are you crazy? I don't smoke.

- I like sports too much to smoke.

- No thanks; I can give you lots of reasons why it's not good for you.

- It doesn't do anything for me.

- "Chicken!" Do you see any feathers on me?

- I like myself just as I am.

- It makes my hair, clothes, and breath smell bad. Why do I want that?

- Are you talking to me? I thought you knew me better.

- I thought you were my friend.

Ticket to Individuality

Do you think that you have to do things that you don't want to in order to be accepted by your friends and classmates? Here's your chance to assert your individuality. On each ticket, write an example of something that you do not want to do to belong to a group.

1. Clothing, hair, or grooming:

Ticket to Individuality

I don't have to _____.

2. Music, TV, radio, video games:

Ticket to Individuality

I don't have to _____.

3. Ways you spend your time or money:

Ticket to Individuality

I don't have to _____.

4. Language:

Ticket to Individuality

I don't have to _____.

Now make four tickets with a characteristic, talent, personality trait, and so forth that would make you feel accepted.

Ticket to Individuality

I would like to be accepted for _____.

Ticket to Individuality

I would like to be accepted for _____.

Ticket to Individuality

I would like to be accepted for _____.

Ticket to Individuality

I would like to be accepted for _____.

Smart Books

Some kids like to keep diaries. Other kids like to draw. Your "Smart Books" give you a chance to do both if you like. We'll be using "Smart Books" to keep up with your smart choices, smart eating habits, and smart exercising habits.

To make your "Smart Books," you can make a booklet or keep a notebook with your favorite color paper. Make it at least 10 pages or more.

Smart Choices

You can use this book to record smart choices or decisions you have made day to day over a month. You can draw pictures or cut out pictures from magazines to illustrate your "smart choices" if you like. You can include smart choices you make at home, school, and in your neighborhood.

Smart Eating

You can use this book to record healthy eating habits over a week or month. Be sure to include a diary of your daily meals, snacks, and water intake. Follow the food pyramid as a guide to making food choices. You may be surprised at your eating patterns and discover you need to make some adjustments to your diet. Once you make adjustments and are eating according to the food pyramid and taking in the proper amount of water, you will probably be surprised at how much better you feel.

Smart Exercising

You can use this book to record healthy exercise habits over a week or month. You may find that doing exercises with a friend will help you stick with this habit, especially at the beginning. Exercise can include what you do in gym class, riding your bike, working in the yard, or doing sit-ups. Again, once you become more conscientious about exercising on a regular basis, you will probably be surprised at how much better you feel.

****

You can keep these books private like a diary or share them with friends, parents or whomever you like. Each time you read your "Smart Books," it will help you feel more confident about the smart choices you have made in your life.

ENERGY

Healthy Body

Self-Esteem

FRIENDS

Role Models

Identity

Faith

Teresea Mathis, Ed.S, LMSW; Susan Smith-Rex, Ed.D.; and Sara Castillo, Ph.D.

Part III

Practical Ideas for Adults to Help

Children Learn What They Live

If a child lives with criticism,
  He learns to condemn.
If a child lives with hostility,
  He learns to fight
If a child lives with ridicule,
  He learns to be shy.
If a child lives with shame,
  He learns to feel guilty.
If a child lives with tolerance,
  He learns to be patient.
If a child lives with encouragement,
  He learns confidence.
If a child lives with praise
  He learns to appreciate.
If a child lives with fairness,
  He learns justice.
If a child lives with security,
  He learns to have faith.
If a child lives with approval,
  He learns to like himself.
If a child lives with acceptance and friendship,
  He learns to find love in the world.

Dorothy Law

Intervention Tools

A Healthy Self-Esteem

A healthy self-esteem is a personal characteristic which is shaped by cultural traditions and social institutions such as families and schools. Therefore, family and school environments play an important part in enhancing self-esteem. Here is some information and ideas to increase self-esteem.

Having a healthy self-esteem places a child in a much less vulnerable position to feel the need to smoke. Along with a healthy self-esteem comes a feeling of peace and well being. These individuals are more able to make good choices, be true friends, and demonstrate positive leadership skills.

Educational literature emphasizes the importance of resilient behavior as it relates to school success and a healthy self-esteem. Part of mastering resiliency is taking part in opportunities that allow us to "come back." Successful resiliency is a reinforcing behavior. When given opportunities to prove you can succeed under adverse conditions, your self-esteem grows and you internalize the ability to feel in control throughout life.

There are five important components to a healthy self-esteem:
1. A feeling of security (at home, at school, and in the neighborhood).
2. A positive identity (feeling noticed for one's strengths and for doing what is expected).
3. A feeling of belonging (emotional link to home and/or school).
4. A sense of purpose (meaningful goals have been identified).
5. A feeling of competence (being good at something one enjoys).

Parents and school personnel can help children develop a healthy self-esteem. Adults should:
1. Set and communicate high expectations.
2. Give caring and insightful feedback.
3. Encourage youngsters to be involved in at least one school/community event (athletic team, club, community service project, or church fellowship group).
4. Help children achieve mastery in something they choose.
5. Set up opportunities for children to give of themselves to others or a cause.
6. Practice good decision-making skills and independent work habits.
7. Establish a personal faith and respect in something greater than oneself.
8. Allow youngsters to be in situations that are challenging enough to fail. If we always protect our children from disappointment, they will remain confident only under ideal conditions. When life hands out adverse conditions, which will happen, they will be inadequately prepared to cope.

9. Give thought to your own adult modeling behavior at times of adversity. Share how you cope when times are tough, and use those moments as "teachable moments." Let children understand the process you use to make "lemonade out of lemons."
10. Schools can use character education or monthly themes school wide.

The following is an example of monthly themes:

Month	Theme/Focus
September	Kindness and Manners—Use table frames with reminders in the cafeteria
October	Making Healthy Decisions—Speakers and activities that focus on 1) Nutrition 2) Exercise 3) Emotional Health 4) Prevention
November	Communications
December	Caring and Sharing
January	Respect
February	Self-awareness
March	Friendship
April	Responsibility
May	Safety

- On the first Monday of each week, have a morning announcement highlighting the theme of the month.
- Have the theme on the marquee.
- Have the classroom and classroom guidance activities focus on the monthly theme.
- Have a special place in the school reserved as a theme wall.
- Provide newsletter information so parents can implement home activities.

Non-smoking education should focus on:

- Responsible behavior
- Decision-making skills
- Improving self-concept
- Building communication skills
- Counseling
- Parenting

Here is how you can go about developing October's Healthy-Decision Making Theme.

1. A Healthy Education Planning Committee needs to be established. (Members of this committee could already be a part of a guidance committee.) Members could include health teachers, the PTO President or designee, the school nurse, an administrator, the librarian, the physical education teacher, the school food service specialist, and the school counselor.

2. Next, this Committee would identify speakers and activities that focus on the areas of nutrition, exercise, emotional health, and prevention. Speakers and activities should be designed to be age-appropriate.

3. Select the dates and the times that the speakers are to come in . Determine who on your committee will contact each speaker.

4. Send confirmation letters to each of your speakers. Within your letter address the following areas: the date, time and location; needs for special audio visual equipment; the number of people they are presenting to; and the name of their student host or hostess. (See a sample letter on page 56.)

5. Send a schedule for the week of "Making Healthy Decisions" to all teachers involved. An example of a schedule used in an elementary school can be found on pages 57 and 58.

6. For middle school and high school, as well as a family night at the elementary level, a Health Fair with representatives from community agencies such as Health Department, Physicians, Dentists, Poison Control, Infection Control, Hospital Nutritionist, Public Safety and MADD could be developed. (Also see page 72 for National Organizations.)

7. Send a thank you note to all participants.

8. Evaluate your program for changes for the following years. Get input from students, teachers, parents, and speakers.

(Letterhead Stationary)

Speaker's Name
Company or Organization
Address
City, State
Zip

Dear_____,

Thank you for volunteering to take part in *school name* Health Awareness Program on *day*, *date*. It is hoped that this letter will help to dispel some of those fears you may be having about now.

Upon arrival, please sign-in in the lobby of our school and you will be greeted by a student host/hostess who will guide you to your individual classroom assignment.

Arrival time: _____

Classroom assignment/Teacher: _____

Time of Sessions: _____

Grade level: _____

Host/Hostess: _____

There will be approximately *number* students in each of your sessions. Each classroom will have a chalkboard, cassette player, screen, and a well-seasoned teacher who can assist you with any needs you may have.

In the past, some of our community resource experts have shared with us what they felt were some of the special "ingredients" used for their successful delivery. These hints may also be helpful to you.

❏ On the board, print your name, occupation, place of employment, and any special words or phrases you may be using in your presentation.

❏ Wear your "uniform" or job appropriate clothing (gloves, hat, boots, and so forth).

❏ Bring any hands-on items or tools used.

❏ Be yourself!

If you have any further questions or concerns, please feel free to contact* name* at *telephone number*. We want to make this as enjoyable for you as we know it will be for our students. We want you to want to come back—often!! Together we can make a difference.

Sincerely,

TO: All teachers

FROM: Guidance Department

RE: Making Healthy Decision Week

School Name will observe *Making Healthy Decisions Week* during *date*. Our focus is to stress to students that *Good Health is in Your Hands.*

Speakers have been invited to visit your classes on *days*. Take this opportunity to stress good health practices. There are videos and supplemental materials available in the library. Please refer to Quest and Character Education notebooks for additional activities. Speaker schedules for the week are as follows:

Grade 1:   *day* and *date*

time in *room assignment*

speaker's name and organization

Grade 2:   *day* and *date*

time in *room assignment*

speaker's name and organization

day and *date*

time in *room assignment*

speaker's name and organization

Grade 3:   *day* and *date*

time in your classrooms

Students will rotate classrooms every 30 minutes

1. **speaker's name and organization**

   Topic

2. **speaker's name and organization**

   Topic

3. **speaker's name and organization**

   Topic

Repeat information for additional grade levels as needed.

In the unfortunate event that a speaker is not able to come, videos will be available to show to your class.

I hope your students enjoy the week's activities.

	Speaker	Room	Teacher	Host/Hostess
Grade 3				
	_____	_____	_____	_____
	_____	_____	_____	_____
	_____	_____	_____	_____
	_____	_____	_____	_____
Grade 4				
	_____	_____	_____	_____
	_____	_____	_____	_____
	_____	_____	_____	_____
	_____	_____	_____	_____
Grade 5				
	_____	_____	_____	_____
	_____	_____	_____	_____
	_____	_____	_____	_____
	_____	_____	_____	_____
Grade 6				
	_____	_____	_____	_____
	_____	_____	_____	_____
	_____	_____	_____	_____
	_____	_____	_____	_____

Teresea Mathis, Ed.S, LMSW; Susan Smith-Rex, Ed.D.; and Sara Castillo, Ph.D.

A Time Line of
Possible Outcomes from Smoking

2 to 18 years	18 to 25 years	25 to 50 years	Over 50
1. Shortness of breath	1. Stained teeth, bad breath, brittle bones	1. Poor physical fitness likely	1. Poor physical fitness likely
2. Heart rate 2 to 3 beats per minute faster	2. More prone to alcohol and drugs	2. Stained teeth, bad breath, brittle bones, wrinkles	2. Stained teeth, bad breath, brittle bones, wrinkles
3. Less likely to participate in sports	3. At risk pregnancy problems: sexual activity, miscarriage, low birth weight, premature baby	3. Increased frequency of respiratory illnesses	3. Increased frequency of respiratory illnesses
4. More likely to struggle with depression	4. Seventy percent wish they never started to smoke	4. Increased risk for lung cancer	4. Increased risk for lung cancer
5. More likely to have emotional complaints		5. Increased risk for stroke	5. Increased risk for stroke
6. Lower self-esteem		6. More prone to alcohol and drugs	6. More prone to alcohol and drugs
7. More likely to be involved in unprotected sex			7. **Eight** years loss in life-span likely
8. Three times more likely to use alcohol			
9. Eight times more likely to use marijuana			
10. Twenty-two times more likely to use cocaine			

Smoking Questionnaire

First name_____ Age _____

What do you think about smoking? _____

What attracts teenagers to smoking? _____

Are you currently a smoker?   ❏ Yes   ❏ No

If you marked "Yes," continue the questions on the front side of this page.

If you marked "No," please answer the questions on page 61.

SMOKERS ONLY

How long have you been smoking? _____

How old were you when you had your first cigarette? _____

What were you doing when you had your first cigarette? _____

Does anyone else in your house smoke? _____

Do your friends smoke? _____

What benefits do you gain from smoking? _____

_____

What physical changes are you noticing because you smoke? _____

_____

Do you think that you are addicted to smoking? _____

Have you tried to stop smoking? _____

Do you plan to be smoking five years from now? _____

Do you experiment with alcohol? _____ Drugs? _____

Do you see a relationship between smoking and other addictive behaviors?_____

Words of advice to help others resist starting to smoke (if you feel that teens should not smoke).

_____

_____

Teresea Mathis, Ed.S, LMSW; Susan Smith-Rex, Ed.D.; and Sara Castillo, Ph.D.

NON-SMOKERS ONLY

If you have tried smoking, but do not currently smoke, please answer the questions below.

How old were you when you were smoking? _____

What were you doing when you smoked? _____

Do your friends smoke? _____

Why did you stop smoking? _____

What made an impact on you to resist this habit? _____

_____

_____

Words of advice to help others resist smoking or to stop if they are already smoking. _____

_____

_____

If you have never tried smoking, please answer the questions below.

Do any of your friends smoke? _____

Do any of your family members smoke? _____

Why did you never try smoking? _____

What has made an impact on you to resist smoking? _____

_____

_____

Words of advice to help others resist smoking or to stop if they are already smoking. _____

_____

_____

What Should Parents Do?

1. Listen, ask, and talk about your child's school day.

2. Be aware of the friends your child spends time with.

3. Watch for any changes in behavior or appearance that concerns you.

4. Encourage your child to get involved in school, church, and community activities and clubs.

5. Keep a written record of your observations concerning your child's behavior.

6. Teach assertive sentences to your child that can help him or her respond assertively to peer pressure.

For example:

- Thanks, but I'm not interested in smoking.

- Sorry, my health is too important to me.

- Are you kidding, it is against the law.

See page 46 for other ways to say no.

What Should Administrators Do?

Consider setting up:

1. A variety of school clubs and encourage all students to join one (drama, cooking, running, photography, art).

2. A workshop for parents on the importance of getting their children involved.

3. A redesign of the playground to increase chances for participation.

4. A school wide, yearlong emphasis on peer support and mediation.

5. A variety of community service projects for students.

6. A few minutes of quiet time each day for students to reflect upon the type of person one respects and admires.

7. Soothing music in the school, when and where appropriate.

8. Ways of providing mentors for children.

9. Suggestions for school board members and Business Partners with requests for support. (Finance a summer leadership program, clubs, and after school programs.)

What Should Teachers Do?

1. Help all students assert themselves regarding their emotional, physical, and mental health.

2. Make anti-smoking posters or collages using magazine pictures and captions.

3. Use a drama club or group to do skits.

What Should Counselors Do?

Where I Stand

To increase the awareness of personal views, make three signs: Agree, Disagree, Don't Know. Place each around the room. The leader reads a statement and students move to the sign that fits their view regarding the statement. Each student should be prepared to explain why he or she chose to stand where he or she is standing. Then discuss what played a part in their decision. For example: Did they move there because their friends did? Are they prepared to stand alone in their decision?

After students are allowed to discuss how they feel about the statement, ask if any want to change their mind. Allow them to move and discuss why they made the move.

Ideas for statements:

- Girls should be allowed to play on all boys sport teams.

- Happiness is something that comes from oneself and not from other people.

- Most of the time there is only one right choice.

- If you start smoking young, you can quit later.

- If you don't inhale smoke, it won't hurt you.

It's My Bag

Give students a brown bag and ask them to put in five or ten items from home that tell something about who the student is. Do not put names on the bags. The next day, the teacher or guidance counselor collects the bags. Each bag is emptied one at a time and students are asked:

- Did a girl or boy bring in the bag?

- How can you tell?

- What kind of activities does this person enjoy?

- Is he or she an indoor person or an outdoor person?

- Why do you think he or she chose these items?

- What one item in the bag do you think he or she is proud of?

Now count to three and have the students point to the person they think belongs to the bag. Allow the person a short amount of time to give a conclusion.

Now go to the next bag!

Get Acquainted with Your Feelings

It is important for kids to know how different situations might make them feel in order to help prepare them to handle future events successfully. The following activity is designed to be done either individually or in a group.

Using a puzzle of your choice, write feeling words on the back of the puzzle pieces. Work the puzzle by discussing the feeling words first and then trying to put the piece in place. The following are some sample discussion questions that can be used to help elicit information from the children.

❏ When is the last time your felt _____ ?

❏ How did that event make you feel?

❏ Was there anything you think you should have done differently?

❏ If so, what?

❏ How would you deal with that situation in the future?

❏ If you handled it differently, how would you feel about yourself?

❏ Would your parents' feelings affect your actions?

❏ Would your friends' feelings affect your actions?

❏ Would your teachers' feelings affect your actions?

Once all the pieces are in place, you can discuss how all feelings are important and that they were all needed to complete the puzzle. The moral to this lesson is knowing how to handle your feelings in a productive manner to help you make good choices. If done in a group, they will also learn the importance of communication to be able to be successful at completing the puzzle. The children will learn that all members of the group contribute to the success of the activity.

Involving Parents

Involving childrens' parents is an essential part to helping children be successful in changing behaviors and making better choices in school. Where appropriate, parents should be an integral part of activities, such as those discussed on pages 41, 42, 46, and 67. Educators, parents, and children working together on these activities to change children's behaviors can improve their self-esteem and develop the possibility for lasting positive relationships.

Educators can help make this happen by linking the activities to home behaviors and rewards. For example, with the *Steps to Success* activity on page 67, parents can be advised of the progress their children are making daily/weekly and provide rewards/incentives to their child to help them reach their ultimate goals. Linking all adults involved in children's lives is the key to helping them be successful at changing behaviors and making good choices.

Jamie Busby

Teresea Mathis, Ed.S, LMSW; Susan Smith-Rex, Ed.D.; and Sara Castillo, Ph.D.

Measuring Your Accomplishments

Puzzle Pieces

In this activity you can help children measure their accomplishments through the use of puzzle pieces. For example, your goal may be to help a child be successful at raising a grade from a "C" to an "A" in any given subject. The puzzle you construct could be a picture of his or her face or anything that would symbolize success to the child. Break this puzzle up into several pieces. With each test or homework assignment where he or she raises a grade, a puzzle piece can be put into place and eventually the picture will be complete.

Mountain of Success

In this activity a mountain climber is used to help measure a child's accomplishment. You can create as many steps as needed for any goal you like, with the end goal being to reach the top of the mountain.

Steps to Success

Attach pictures of students or characters to clothespins. Move the clothespin characters up the ladder with each step measuring success. When they reach the top of the ladder, they have met their goal and should celebrate!

Touchdowns, Goals, Baskets, etc.

Various sports can be used to help children measure their accomplishments. Depending on the time of year, you may use football, soccer, basketball, and so forth. Let's say you use football touchdowns to measure success. You can define what types of behaviors qualify as touchdowns. For example, saying no to smoking. Then after a predetermined number of touchdowns are achieved, they can be cashed in for a reward.

• •

On the following page is a SEAL of Approval Certificate. Here are some examples of how the certificate can be used:

❑ Student organizations such as the Student Council or the Just Say No Club can award the certificate to members.

❑ The PTO and student representatives could award the certificate to community businesses who support not selling tobacco products to minors.

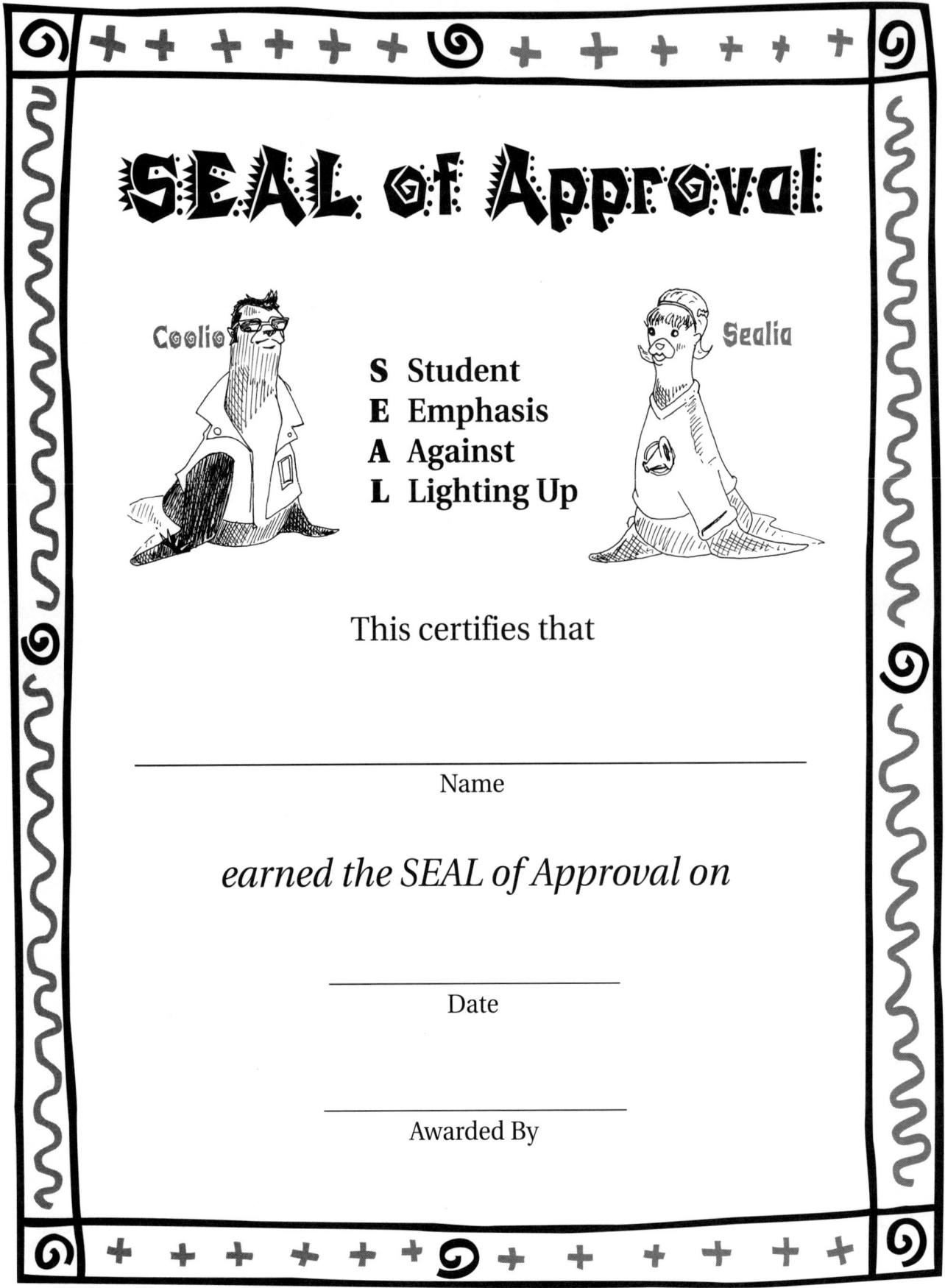

SEAL of Approval

Coolio

Sealia

S Student
E Emphasis
A Against
L Lighting Up

This certifies that

_____
Name

earned the SEAL of Approval on

_____
Date

_____
Awarded By

Coolio

Chris Gervais

Chris Gervais

Teresea Mathis, Ed.S, LMSW; Susan Smith-Rex, Ed.D.; and Sara Castillo, Ph.D.

References

Americans for Nonsmokers' Rights. (1997). *Tobacco smoke and the non-smoker.* Berkeley, CA: Author.

Buttheads. (1998, October). *Topics Magazine,* Vol. 4, No. 3, Charlotte, NC.

Capital Region Healthy Kids Center. (1992). *Healthy kids tobacco-free workshop guide.* Sacramento, CA: California Department of Education.

DiFranza, et al. (1991). R.J.R. Nabisco's cartoon camel promotes Camel Cigarettes to children. *Journal of the American Medical Association,* 266:22, 3149-3153.

Feighery, E., Altman, D.G., & Shaffer, G. (1991). The effects of combining education and enforcement to reduce tobacco sales to minors. *Journal of the American Medical Association,* 266:22, 3168-3171.

Fisher, P.M., Schwartz, M.P., Richards, J.W., Golstein, A.O., & Rojas, T.H. (1991). Brand logo recognition by children aged 3 to 6 years. *Journal of the American Medical Association,* 266:22, 3145-3148.

Lew, J. (1991). Cracking down on stores that sell cigarettes to children. *Tobacco on trial.* Boston, MA: Northeastern University School of Law.

Pierce, J.P., et al. (1991). Does tobacco advertising target young people to start smoking: Evidence from California. *Journal of the American Medical Association,* 266:22, 3154-3158.

Sarason, I.G., et al. (1992). Adolescent reasons for smoking. *Journal of School Health.*

Smokin'. (1999, November 28). *The Herald.*

Taylor, C.B., & Killen, J.D. (1991). *The facts about smoking.* Yonkers, NY: Consumer Reports Books.

The psychological triggers of tobacco. (1999). Mt. Kisco, NY: HRM Video.

Tobacco marketing: Profiteering from children. (1991). *Journal of the American Medical Association,* 266:22, 3185-3189.

US Department of Health and Human Services. (1994). *Preventing tobacco use among young people: A report of the surgeon general.* Washington DC: US Government Printing Office. (Publication number 017-001-00491-0).

National Organizations

American Cancer Society (National Bureau)
    1599 Clifton Road, NE
    Atlanta, GA 30329
    (800) ACS-2345 or check in your local phone directory for regional office

American Heart Association (National Bureau)
    7320 Greenville Avenue
    Dallas, TX 75231
    (214) 750-5300 or check in your local phone directory for regional office.

American Lung Association (National Bureau)
    1740 Broadway
    New York, NY 10019-4374
    (212)315-8700 or check in your local phone directory for regional office.

Americans For Nonsmokers' Rights
    2530 San Pablo, Suite J
    Berkeley, CA 94702

Centers For Disease Control And Prevention (Cdcp)
    Office on Smoking and Health
    5600 Fishers Lane
    Park Building, Room 1-16
    Rockville, MD 20857   (301)443-5287

National Cancer Institute
    9000 Rockville Pike
    Building 31, Room 4A-18
    Bethesda, MD 20892   (800)4-CANCER

Nicotine Anonymous (National Office)
    2118 Greenwich Street
    San Francisco, CA 94123

    Check your local phone book under "Associations" or
    "Social and Human Services" for the nearest meeting center.

Smoke-Free Schools
    1680 Duke Street
    Alexandria, VA 22314

STAT (Stop Teenage Addiction To Tobacco)
    511 E. Columbus Avenue
    Springfield, MA 01105   (413)732-7828